SINGLE AND LOVING IT

Simple Practical Guides To Finding Joy And Peace In Singleness

Kim Gary

CONTENTS

INTRODUCTION

"When are you getting married?"

"Do you know you are not getting younger, when is your marriage holding?"

These were the questions I usually got and more when I was single. It got to a stage I thought about just going on a random date, even though I already decided to work on me more before I would start any relationship. During this period, it felt like I would not be able to be single for the duration I needed to work on myself, that the loneliness will be overwhelming, but I said to myself "I can do this and I will come out stronger", and I did, but it was not easy. You taking this decision will have its own rough path but it will be one of the best decisions you make.

when you're moving alone, it can seem like the entire world is enamored with being in love, and everybody around you is fixated on why you're not collaborating up and siphoning out kids. And keeping in mind that you need to let them know where to go or shout, you realize you have to keep the harmony because you're not that individual.

Be that as it may, truly, it tends to be super-irritating when individuals feel like it's their obligation to push you out of the "single" enclose and to the "taken" box. What's more, it very well may be much harder to meet somebody, yet you simply haven't associated with the right one yet.

Despite the fact that it might feel like the end is close to given all that is continuing, it's not the apocalypse since you're single. This moment really is a very decent opportunity to place things in context, deal with yourself and figure out what you truly ask for from a relationship assuming that is what you genuinely want.

Some single people often complain that they are alone, this is not so. They have companions around them like friends, relatives. They have gatherings and they have work, they have heaps of connections. They simply don't have a better half. Along these lines, they're in good company. They're only not in a close connection. What's more, I think single individuals experience a great deal of cultural strain. In any case, assuming that is what you want and you're blissful, who's to say that is not all right?"

CHAPTER ONE

Is It Strange To Be Single?

Continually being examined concerning being distant from everyone else could cause you to feel like something is off about you. It additionally doesn't help when it appears as though there's another self-improvement relationship book or unscripted TV drama coming out each and every other day. In spite of what you see or hear, being single isn't strange.

Some people often said being single is not normal, this is not true, being single is very normal. In any case, there is a lot of stigmas attached to being single and quite a bit of it is by all accounts cultural. "Network shows, online media, and even stories we read as kids could likewise add to certain individuals' negativity with being single.

"What's more, the fantasies we read as youngsters make them search for our better half, so we can live joyfully ever later," However, assuming you're OK with being single and you're blissful, who's to say that is not all right?"

When Asked Why You Are Still Single
It's Inescapable

Certain individuals will hit you with this inquiry. Furthermore, when they do, remember that you genuinely don't owe them a clarification. Try not to rationalize sentiments for why you're actually single. Whenever you do this, it's like you're discounting yourself.

"We can't oversee others' tension with regards to what's the deal with us. All things being equal, when they inquire as to why you're single, you can grin and say, things are fine, We should discuss you,' and change the subject"

Individuals will have tension with regards to what you do or don't do, however, you don't need to acknowledge it, you don't need to become tied up with it and you don't need to feel remorseful.

"Whenever we begin rationalizing why we're not in a relationship or why we're single, we simply propagate the possibility that couples are great and being single isn't. Being single or in a relationship is fine, yet it, at last, comes down to what in particular works for every person."

Is There Justification For Why You Are Still Single?

We should be our number one priority, if you do not contend in yourself first who will? In the event that you're not content with yourself or content with your present circumstance, bouncing into a relationship won't improve things.

Having strong confidence in yourself can assist with being prepared for a relationship or being happier with being single. Both are positive results. To assist with placing things into point of view and to sort out what you need, ponder the justifications for why you're single and ask these questions:

Assuming you are content generally, are there outside pressures that cause you to feel lacking?

In the event that you are not happy with being single, what do you need in a relationship?

Where are you hoping to track down this individual?

Might it be said that you are effectively seeking after a relationship or sitting tight for it to fall into your lap?

Assuming you've had a fruitless relationship, what made them be like that? Is there something that you need to chip away at with regards to your own characteristics?

CHAPTER TWO

How Figuring Out How To Appreciate Being Single Can Make You More Joyful

Here are the advantages of being agreeable single and how you can construct this expertise to yourself for more inner harmony and happiness:

1 If You Can't Be Cheerful Single, You Can't Be Blissful In A Relationship

On the off chance that you should be with others to feel content, you'll attempt to look for bliss from things outside of you - things which you have positively zero influence over. It additionally implies you want others for your joy, which compels you to stick and do things you typically wouldn't do.

This issue has large outcomes. Some people, because of the fear of being single will settle for less. In this situation, the apprehension about being separated from everyone else impacts individuals to settle on helpless choices and pick any individual rather than the right individual.

"Looking for a relationship to ease our discontent with ourselves is a pointless undertaking. We should initially figure out how to be on our own from everyone else, then, at that point, and really at that time would we be able to be a decent partner to another person. In light of the fact that then we can search for a relationship since we want to, and not out of a need to feel total.

Being in a relationship is not an answer for an individual issue, a relationship represents a totally different arrangement of issues on its own. Assuming you find that you have been considering a relationship the solution for your life, look somewhere else to fulfill your despondency, check it out yourself, and start to manage your issues.

And if eventually, you start a relationship, that shock of energy may blur after some time. Whenever we get something and feel blissful, we will quite often adjust and lose that happiness then we attempt to get something different, and the cycle rehashes.

Likewise, in the event that you can't be cheerful without a relationship, then, at that point, each relationship disappointment, from terrible dates to separations, will wreck you. Why surrender your joy?

Being "on your own from everyone else" is not the same as being "forlorn:" One is what is happening while the other is an assessment of that circumstance.

2. How Being Blissful Alone Can Give You Opportunity

Would the right relationship be able to improve and enhance your life? Obviously! Having extraordinary companionships and relationship has gigantic advantages. Yet, being agreeable and certain without anyone else, permits you to appreciate others in a confined manner. Rather than hoping for relationship, companions, dates, as the principal wellspring of your joy, or a method for keeping away from the aggravation and shame of being alone from everyone else, but you give your own joy and self-esteem, which prompts more satisfying relationship and friendship.

You can deliberately pick individuals you appreciate rather than sticking to the individuals who chose you, and you can even relinquish individuals, relationships, and accomplices unafraid.

Additionally, by wiping out the tension of being single, you can accomplish more exercises without anyone else, which can open new open doors that were incomprehensible without it.

Why You Should Change Your Attitude About Being Single

To Start With, being single is a decision. In the event that you want to, practically every one of you reading this could be in a relationship now. However, you'd most likely need to forfeit your freedom, guidelines.

Understanding that your singleness is a decision, it can decrease sensations of nervousness, depression, or instability. One of the most well-known justifications for why individuals are single is they need the opportunity to do what they what and prioritize other things.

Second, being single doesn't mean you "fizzled." Many individuals get disturbed that they make a decent attempt and still can't find a partner. Yet, you can't handle each part of your dating life-here and there, it's simply a mix of timing and luck.

Also assuming you only possibly feel fruitful when you're seeing someone and you put your self-esteem, joy, and character on it - the result won't be great.

"Disappointment" in dating isn't being single; it's being in an awful relationship with a terrible partner. All things considered, being in a poisonous relationship causes something other than hurt sentiments: It prompts higher pressure rates, heart issues, circulatory strain, and even weight. What's more, not all relationships you see are blissful.

Lastly, a relationship shouldn't give you joy; you ought to give your own joy. Relationship simply gives you another person to impart your bliss on.

CHAPTER THREE

Different Ways Being Single Can Work On Your Life

Being single isn't generally a stroll in the park- particularly when films and TV programs appear to push the idea that you're not genuinely "complete" until you've viewed it as a better half.

Individuals' single lives are regularly depicted as a kind of limbo they are compelled to suffer until they observe their perfect partners. Also, those solitary individuals are regularly remembered to be despondent by others.

Be that as it may, these couldn't possibly be more off-base. Truth be told, it is found that solitary individuals self-detailed degrees of prosperity that was like members seeing someone. Also, there are a lot of advantages that show up with carrying on with your life liberated from a close connection.

1. Your Mind Is Free

"Closeness and association occupy a ton of room in our minds. Despite the fact that a lot of this is occurring unknowingly, there's just a lesser limit with regards to the separately engaged idea."

There are times individuals spend definite agonizing time worrying over their partner and, on occasion, ruminating on even the littlest fights, as "the cost of affection." This kind of stress can restrain individuals' satisfaction by holding them back from living in them at this point. Being single is a demonstration of cleansing the messiness and accounting for groundbreaking contemplations (and dreams) to inhale and develop,"

2. You're More Open To Anything That Life Tosses Your Direction

Being single can make individuals more ready to adapt to all challenges

Liberated from the imperatives of having a partner, individuals' lives out of nowhere become absolutely and totally their own, there's no one upsetting you from embarking to pursue your desires. "You're bound to face challenges and have undertakings and be more curious in your excursion.

3. Have The Opportunity To Reach Out To Yourself

"Individuals say a ton of times, when they're seeing someone, that they've lost themselves", and that is to a great extent since we quit doing things freely."

When in a relationship, some individuals rarely move away from on their own since they have less time alone to zero in on their very own events. "At the point when you're not involved with anyone, it sets out freedom for being more in contact with something within you,"

The normal grievance heard from individuals seeing someone is that they're feeling withdrawn from their innovative sides. Whenever you're single, there's more space for creativity" and time to focus on it more.

4. You Get An Opportunity To Sort Out What You Truly Desire

When you are not in a relationship, you have some an ideal opportunity to get clear with what is important to and what you hold in esteem. That is the point at which you can look back and consider lessons gained from past relationships. "Being single is the ideal opportunity to reconsider what your identity is and where you need to be throughout everyday life. What do you want to create? You presently have the opportunity and the capacity to zero in on the one predictable element that will make the change, no doubt about it."

5. You Develop A Nonromantic Relationship

While romantic relationships are regularly focused on, solid kinships are unquestionably significant. Whenever you have the opportunity and space to really focus on them, they can advance our lives incomparable and surprisingly better ways than romantic ones. Whenever we're single, we truly will generally have more opportunities to have time with ourselves and other significant relationships.

6. It Can Tend To Be The Most Ideal Situation

Seeing someone can be the ideal decision at all times for everybody. "But being single and cheerful seems like the main reasonable choice for somebody who's searching for affection and isn't tracking down it."

To genuinely turn out to be joyfully single, practice care. "Such a large amount of bliss has to do with living right now," doing this will improve different parts of your life, as well. You can get clear on what's critical to you, you have a tons of opportunity. You can plan your greatest day," "Assuming you're investing your single energy ruminating concerning how you will meet somebody, the matter is up you alone to decide on.

7. Developing And Extending Nonromantic Connections

While heartfelt relationships are regularly focused on, solid kinships are unquestionably significant. Whenever we have the opportunity and space to really focus on them, they can advance our lives incomparable and surprisingly better ways than heartfelt ones. Being single will truly help to generally have more opportunity to zero in on yourselves and other significant relationships.

8. It's An Opportunity To Turn Out To Be Financially Capable

One of the advantages individuals regularly characterize to a relationship is the capacity for the two partners to share liabilities and monetary weights. Being single can really boost you to be more parsimonious and monetarily autonomous.

"Here and there when you're single and don't impart costs to another person, you drive yourself to progress and to be creative on the grounds that you're not depending on another person to cover your costs. This can be something incredible for your profession and life.

9. Focus On Taking Care Of Yourself

"Being in a relationship can be brilliant. "We have somebody with whom to share our promising and less promising times, as they do with us. In any case, when we're single, we're expected to zero in on the aspects of our lives that need attention"

For example, working out, associating with our partner, "investing in some opportunity to zero in on private goals, and investing energy alone, regularly get shoved aside when in a relationship in the midst of our need to help others. "While single, there's no interruption that pulls us from taking care of ourselves and self-improvement.

10. You Figure Out How To Appreciate Your Own Company

Being single shouldn't really be inseparable from being forlorn. You can acquire an appreciation for time alone, it is freeing.

"Being content in our own organization liberates us from the need to pursue others."

Whenever we figure out how to appreciate being separated from everyone else, we become more particular with regards to the organization we pick investing energy with just the people who work on our lives and add to our prosperity, and development.

11. Your Confidence Level Can Soar

"Whenever you're separated from everyone else, there's a strength that nearly must be there. "We quite often here and there depend on our partner for much" but, being single gives a valuable chance to take advantage of one's inward assets, which can really appear in a more noteworthy degree of certainty.

CHAPTER FOUR

Step-By-Step Instructions To Be Content Single.

1. Focus On Association

At the point when single, you may be more proactive about interfacing with individuals in your day-to-day existence, however, it's worth the effort. "Social association is plainly connected with psychological well-being, and seclusion/disengagement unavoidably prompts encountering nervousness and gloom.

2. Date Yourself

Think about this as when you get to date yourself, be your own partner, and give yourself all the affection you would anticipate from a partner (and that you would provide for them). Get yourself gifts, take yourself out, buy yourself flowers, and center all this on you. Put effort into investing in some opportunity to sort out what you truly need throughout everyday life, getting to 'date' yourself is a magnificent chance.

3. Join Gatherings, Take Classes, Or Start A Side Hustle

Make the most of having free nights and ends of the week and not working around another person's timetable," Regardless of whether that is a painting course, a sporting games association, or plunging into that side hustle, you have the amazing chance to zero in on anything you desire. It's a potential chance to investigate new side interests and things that give you pleasure.

4. Make And Invest Energy With A Single Companion

Making new, single companions can help your emotionally supportive network with individuals who can connect with your present conditions. Having few friends to share words and whom you can connect with at all levels is a plus and it will go a long way.

5. Zero In On Your Own Taking Care Of Yourself

Whenever you're single, "You can zero in on your own taking care of yourself without worrying about offsetting it with your partner." Anything taking care of oneself looks like to you, from working out to getting out into nature, truly focus on it.

6. Find Out With Regards To Yourself

"Practice self-request and self-sympathy. At the point when you invest in some opportunity to find out with regards to yourself, you can get clear on what you need from yourself and your life. Find out with regards to your connection style, your feelings, and your internal voice, and maybe even work with a specialist or mentor "to see how you may be keeping yourself away from making the existence you need and merit."

7. Be Unconstrained

Being single accompanies a lot of opportunities. Accordingly, appreciate being

more at liberty with your exercises and travel."
"You can genuinely pick where you need to go or what you need to do as a person. There is a great deal of opportunity when you are single to plan the sort of life you need to make.

8. Put Objectives And Energy Into Your Development

Being single allows us an opportunity to really consider ourselves responsible, support ourselves, and settle on our own choices and objectives. Utilize this opportunity to get clear on what you need to accomplish, regardless of whether it's private, monetary, and so on. Think about how far you've come each time you arrive at another objective.

9. Keep Viewpoint

It's essential to keep the point of view when single, to try not to get down on yourself for what can be a brilliant time of your life. Remind yourself:

I'm on my own mending venture, and my future partner is on theirs too. They're accomplishing the work to be the individual I want them to be in their relationship, I'm doing likewise. At the point when everything looks good, we'll meet up to proceed with our journey.

10. You Won't Always Be Single If You Don't Want To Be

To get into a relationship sometime in the not-so-distant future, then, at that point, it's probably going to come around ultimately. When planning to get into a relationship, should it be sooner or later, keep in mind that relationship can be great.

CHAPTER FIVE

CONCLUSION

Whether or not you are single, we alone merit our own self-esteem and organization. At the point when you can like being single and utilize an opportunity to fortify your self-appreciation, your value, and get clear on what you truly need, the advantages will swell in all aspects of your life. Relationships are brilliant, yet nothing beats being on your own for a change, especially if you are not being appreciated or not finding happiness, appreciating your own conversation, and adoring precisely what your identity is, single or not.

"The best relationship happens when you have a decent comprehension of your necessities, needs, and values. Being single permits you to zero in on these things. Having this certainty and mindfulness will, at last, serve you in your relationship as a whole, not only romantic ones."